NO MAN'S LAND

First published in 2023 by
The Dedalus Press
13 Moyclare Road
Baldoyle
Dublin D13 K1C2
Ireland

www.dedaluspress.com

ISBN 978-1-915629-21-0 (paperback)
ISBN 978-1-915629-20-3 (hardback)

Dedalus Press titles are available in Ireland
from Argosy Books (www.argosybooks.ie) and in the UK
from Inpress Books (www.inpressbooks.co.uk).

Cover artwork: *My Sunday* (16cm x 16cm), organic cotton
mull on linen/cotton blend and embroidery floss,
by Ana Galindo, by kind permission of the artist.
Instagram *@fibreartsatelier.*

Dedalus Press receives financial assistance from
The Arts Council / An Chomhairle Ealaíon.

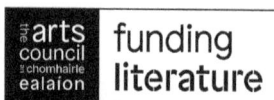

the arts council
chomhairle ealaíon
funding
literature

NO MAN'S LAND

DAVID NASH

DEDALUS PRESS

ACKNOWLEDGEMENTS

The first thing I'd like to acknowledge, given the kind of thing that follows in this book, is where it was written, under whose roofs, and thanks to whose generosity. First, then, to my parents, Liam and Siobhán, and their/my/our home in Canovee, County Cork. The people and the place are inextricable, and I cannot believe my luck in being born to both. Haunted too (in the Cork sense) with my siblings, Joanne, Billy, Eimear, and Mary: many of these poems were hammered out while walking to, from and around their houses, and they wouldn't have been if those houses hadn't always been so open to me.

Other locations where poems were so kindly allowed to form: the homes of: Anne-Marie and Laura Connolly-McGann; Alexander Dudley and Isobella Rafty; Laurence Avis and Sarah Stallbohm; David Ring and Harriet Waldegrave; Marcella Creedon; Olaf Boswijk and Mirla Klein; and Chloé Billebault and Vicente Rosati.

Two residencies, one in the Burren College of Art in Ballyvaughan, and the other at Valley of the Possible in Cañon del Blanco, can stake a legitimate claim to a good third or so of this book. I don't know how to express gratitude for having a world opened to me. Maybe by returning.

More gratitude again to Tom Ironmonger, Jessica Dehen, Mícheál McCann, Nevada Street Poets, Suzanne Ní Bhriain and Stephen O'Shea, for spotting things, teaching things, and cleaning things up.

Many of these poems, or iterations of them, have appeared in *Poetry Ireland Review, 14 Poems, Queer Anthology Series, Propel, Impossible Archetypes, Cork Words, Copihue Review,* and the Dedalus Press *Local Wonders* anthology.

The editor of the latter, Pat Boran, is the editor of this very book too, and I thank him here for his patience, keen eye, and kindness.

Go raibh maith agaibh – very literally – *go léir.*

Contents

Do mo neachtanna agus nianna:
go mbeadh foighne agaibh le bhur ndúchas.

Man braucht nicht viel Besonderes zu sehen.
Man sieht so schon viel.
— Robert Walser, *Kleine Wanderung*

Nettle

I'd like to bring my grandfather back to life just to get him stoned,
the good kind, the thirst and laughter kind. He had, I think,
    kind laughter.
My plan is this: I'd tell him the weed was nettle seeds I'd honed
to be smokeable, we'd use his pipe. *I hope twon't kill me*, he'd
    say, *and me just after*
dying. But I am his. People of his don't do him harm, we're
    reliable as clothing.
I'd watch him reinhabit his trout-skin, retake stock of his own
    mouth,
suck his false tooth like he used, laugh about this. I need to
    know some things.
Did being called Gaga put in or put out on him? Is it true that
    in this part of the south

they used to make known their love by whipping the object of
    it with a nettle?
True, Gaga would tell me, *the grasping of the stinger was the pain*
    that proved it.
Here he'd open his big bready hands and stroke out the lines
    where the leaves should settle.
Gentleness won't work. It should be in your hand before it knows
    you've moved it.
He'd fix his bloodshot eyes on Granny's masscard, curling on
    the shelf.
He'd tell me all of this. I wouldn't have to find out for myself.

Alamos

When they scroll past on long bus journeys, I can translate them into any caliber of metaphor – cardiograph of the country, cloud-scourers, bird-botherers, nature's cuneiform, village gossips, barcode of the sky - but never into English. I forget and I'm stumped – I wish there was another word for it.

This is for the best, since they are terrible. They have this knack of splintering into my life when I am at my loneliest and least beautiful, erect when I am bonelessness incarnate. I'd rather not give them the benefit of memory and know them by heart, being as they are the iffiest of masts, the middlest of fingers; trying their damnedest, as they do, never to touch one another.

Lámh

I've been having a hard time lately.
For a few minutes of relief

I learn to cup my upraised elbow in my palm
then turn and return my free open hand, as if I am

picking an orange whose circumference only
I can discern: that's how you say *tree*.

When I perform this later on FaceTime for Aisling,
she forgoes the sign for applause, in favour of the real thing.

Imaginary Farmer

You don't know shit, says my imaginary farmer
when we have debates about reducing the national herd.
*Literally, like. You don't know the first thing
about it. Not the gleaming cakes the cows leave
in their wake, not the ripe road-apples of the coach horse,
not the rat-slick, not the castings of the worms, earth's
afterbirth, not the stuff people are happy as pigs in,
not bunny bullets, not spraint, not frass, not scat, not fewmets.
Not squat. You wouldn't know the dropping from the bird that drops it.*
(He is something of a poet himself, of course,
and uses lists as shock-and-awe.)
I do though, I protest. *Couldn't I tell you your future
from the pattern of the cracks in week-old lorum,
which, by the way, is bespoke Nash family vocab for cow-pats?
And don't I know my own? And am I not an alchemist myself,
like every other beast? Do you think you're above or apart from it?*
And we go on like this, knowing things at each other
while gravity draws every step closer in to land
and all our eyes roll heavenwards.

Snow Drop

Out
in breathless space
the universe
is testing

its own waistband.
This is where we have
got to:
at any given time

a twirl-cum-hurtle,
still though
it might seem.
Arms of sun-

fuss gesture
to the offshoots
circling, thus
blessing them

with light, though
really light is an
afterthought. A tangent –
mathematics

comes into it – skims
the Earth, and it's
winter,
since its back was

turned at the time.
Plates of air
hover over the world like
a gypsywoman's hands,

closer in more
like loose satsuma rind.
The sea
is water

that rides on the shoulders
of other water.
North-north-west
of Donegal,

it happens
to be warm over cold
ascending.
For these and other reasons

I don't get, snow
won't fall in
my part of this
country. I

see these ersatz
flowers now like hangovers,
above ground but still
ground-facing,

pangs of light,
like those pre-sleep
alarm-bells
that sometimes

ring: what might have
been, what might
have been, what
might have been.

A Day at the Beach

There's a wall chart for the new Gaeilgeoirí
that loads a beach with impossible
numbers of animals and geographies, an allegory
maybe for what we don't have and aren't able
to say. An *abhainn* makes two arcs unfettered.
There's a neat *oileán*, some *deilfeanna ag snámh*.
Crab and cliff and seahorse are remade in words
as bright and artless as new love.

What's left to be desired:
the slap of wet shorts on rock,
more unprotected skin than
we know what to do with.
Humans at the beach are animal
in the best way – all movement is
the least effort for the most reward,
and from hunger to fullness
is as the crow flies. The poster is right
to show words and not grammar.
At the beach there's no grammar, no restraint.

On Seeing My Sister Plant Three Trees for her Children

I

It's tempting fate to thumb
a seed into the earth
and make it happen,
to have it found the business
of itself, incurring debts
to nitrogen and phosphorous
and leave it to acquaint itself
with rain
and from rain somehow benefit.

You think yourself
a bearess, a protectress of terrain,
but what the earth sees fit
to cancel, what voice to strike dumb,
it will. The earth
is competition:
it has no business
judging a life on its merits,
that this tree here deserves to prosper

and that one there should bear witness
to the lucklessness of death.
Nitrogren, phosphorous,
water, air and light exchange themselves
within a living thing, sometimes in vain.
That's the size of it.
Still you tempted fate, and thumbed
a seed into the earth
and made it happen. Again, and then again.

II

Since I won't be a father to anyone, I'll say this:
I wish you never to hear your own heart
beat into the mattress, bed frame, beat across the floor,
advance throughout the house with the thirst of electricity,
making sing its starscape of nails,
and then slink back along those same branches of electricity,
back through beams and doorways, back across the floor,
come back empty-handed, the heartbeat returning to the father-heart.
I wish you anything, anything but this.

The Plastic Bag Full of Plastic Bags under the Sink

You know you're Irish if you have one of these,
though you'll also find you're Armenian
or Hispanic or Jewish or Czech, because thrift
is universal. What, then, is Irish? Is it Dansk

biscuit tins full of sewing detritus? Not ours
either? Stew is also out – it isn't really an
innovation to boil all the food that you have left,
or at least not one so easily claimed. To ask

an old lad on the road directions, shoot the breeze
and end up drinking with him? #onlyinireland?
The past is better everywhere, and there's no craft
in protesting so much difference. But there is risk.

Not

Another culture might not have paid mind, but mine
caught on, or got caught, and made the following of the blackthorn:
inventories of luck and unluck; line after line
of instruction and warning; knowledge not to know, but to perform
here, on the stage of the supernatural; gauge
of the work we put into winter; hex; diuretic; summer's betrayal;
easer of mastitis, therefore summoner of cream; hedge-
queen; bread substitute; comedy to fairy-folk; catastrophe to fell.

What, might ask the blackthorn, has all this crap to do with me?
I'm a tree. I suck the earth and cast off seeds as rent.
If I should bend towards you, it doesn't mean you're meant
for me, or that in this there's meaning. Patriot,
land-love is a one-way street, and so is land-anxiety.
The eye of this wood is not its eye. It is its knot.

Hy Brasil

The island can be found if the ship can see the island before the island the ship [...] And it is small and round and flat.
—Lope García de Salazar, *Libro de Bienandanzas e Fortunas,* 1492

after Seán Ó Riordán's 'Saoirse'

If it can be anything, let it be empty.
If I can be anything on it, let me either be empty
or completely full, just so long as
I'm not always finding these spaces inside myself.

On Hy Brasil I'm dumb as muck.
If we must still grade flesh, then I'm chum.
As far as insight goes, it doesn't.

I come only with the shirt on my back
and even that seems overkill. There is,
in fact, no Hy Brasil
Fashion Week. I wear not what
but if I want.

One day out of every seven
years there is light; the rest is mist,
which fills in for sky. That's fine with me:
I've reached ennui for wow-inducing mountains
and far-as-the-eye-can-sees.

As for words, I don't see why
they'd be needed.

There are no golf courses on Hy Brasil.
The Old Head of Kinsale is reproduced there in full,

unpreened, unbunkered and unbored by men;
my father plays a different sport
on a different island.

I don't fiddle with packaging
anymore. Every password I have
stuffed into the sausage-casing
of my brain can rot with the
flotsam of the boat that sails me here.
My body now is password enough.
No one need ask me for proof
I'm human

and speaking of bodies, let mine not need feeding,
so Thomasina Miers' recipe for
honey-roast quince salad with blue cheese, radicchio
    and seared venison
can stay snug in its book
and leave me alone.

My Hy Brasil is Beckett-play barren
or real Brazil lush. I don't mind.
Just let its fertility or infertility
not be politics.
I do not keep abreast
and am not kept abreast
of any movements, shifts, schisms
or splicings, because current affairs are
what drove me here.

There are no cinemas on Hy Brasil.
Don't ask me what I've seen
if somehow you see me.

In the money exchange of thought,
I don't even want the coins – let alone
the notes. Hy Brasil is cashless,
odourless, sexless, and bare.

I'll let my brother come on the one clear day in every seven
years, to see what else I've disallowed, and say
Jesus, Dave there's not much else left, is there?
just so that I can say back to him
Well, Billy, that might just be what I'm after.

rip.ie

So now I place the notice on RIP
and carry out its grammar – you can either
say *after a long illness borne with dignity*
or *passed unexpectedly*; then who survives him; then where

he will be woken. Women called Gobnait or Assumpta
ask their daughters to bring up the page, and are, sincerely,
sorry. Some write only to be seen to write, some to
get a vote come next election, some leave the surname box empty.

There's humour, yes, between the sentiment and the medium.
There's help in knowing others have known death,
and not just of a life. There's gossip too –
that's most likely where language came from.
The site says *Condolences become Read Only after a month*,
but by then the word will have got out, as words tend to.

river(s)

Should any of us drown (our young, our best even) the river must be considered to have carried out its duty.

When the river has had it up to here with us, it will point out to sea.

If a river is cold, it does not know it is cold. Only we know that.

Between the flower picked and the flower given: this is the length of a river.

These are the colours a river can be: blue; black; off-blue; universe blue; the colour of an orange; rain black; rain brown; home-, love-, folksong blue.

The river doesn't laugh from the mouth. It laughs from the mountain.

What if the river, after all this time, would really rather not be water?

Wake me, world, when you've decided on one word for river; on the grading of a river; on what sex a river is.

Falling is the lot of rivers.

By the dam on the river they purify water. Think: to bring water back to itself; every day to say water, and write water. Not just to imply it.

I am a river, and I have undertaken to say so in words: I am a work of translation.

Life is a river. Time is a river. Love? Love is a river. Achievement? People? Rivers.
The river as metaphor *is* metaphor.

Do you pass the last bend and forget, river, or must you know it and know it again?

The curriculum of the river is this, in no particular order: geography, music, its own country's language, physics, history, classics, foreign languages, religion.

If there were a hierarchy of waters, the river would be king and serf in one – calling the shots, and doing the shooting.

The first word is water, and the last word is water. What the river says, goes.

Forget-me-not

How could I, dear,
    when you've held so fast down there in the sedge,
    seeing as how you've ridden out the slow sex of river on shore,
    given you've gone blue, gone pink, yellowed or whitened
    according to what the pollinators might be looking for that day,
    considering the cuckoo spits on you, none other,
        remembers you and spits on you yearly,
    bearing in mind how much it takes, in spite of ruin and
        the eyes of humans, to live life as a flower among flowers,
    in view of your place in the breast pocket of language,
    taking your centre into account, your yellow bellybutton,
        iris, anus, desire of men;
    given how you've pushed yourself on them,
    in light of all this, apropos of effort, being as you're still here,
    since everything you do is so as not to be forgotten?

Flights

"Happy families resemble one another; every unhappy family is
unhappy in its own way"
— Tolstoy

Seeing as it's the preserve of those who are grieving, and one
serious perk of grief, to have all art suddenly be about oneself, I
am taking the above to have been written about me. To be more
specific, I'm taking it to have been written about me and all the
birds of my life, and more specifically again about the manner in
which they have flown out of it. How they are all only birds, all
just called 'bird', when I'm not there to observe them or be
observed by them, but how then, on sight, they scatter, and in
scattering define themselves; as if my shadow could slice the
whole class into genus, sub-genus, species.

It's not unusual for certain things to be clearer in departure
than in presence, or clearer in death than in life, or, as with
Tolstoy above, clearer in misery than in joy. Even with the best
will in the world, once the steak has gone from mouth to
stomach, it's the aftertaste the carnivore is left with. What you
feel when the film ends will tell you what it meant; then you step
back out into the world, imperceptibly other than when you
stepped in. All goodbyes, from the limpest to the firmest
handshake, somehow manage to capsulise the relationships
they're sealing.

And so it is with birds, who have only ever told me who they
are in flight.

29

So I am applying what Leo Tolstoy wrote 150-odd years ago about unfaithfulness and desire to myself and the snipe. On one of those close days where the clouds appear to be within the range of a skimming stone, I was was standing at the lip of the lake and something shot out from the reeds and across the water like accidental gunfire: unmeant, but unmistakable. That was the first I ever knew of a snipe. I described it in an embarrassing way to my uncle Phil, who used to hunt duck when there were still duck on the lake, and who I knew could at least tell one feathered thing from another: it was the colours more or less of a latte, I said, and about the size of a latte mug. He took the piss out of me of course, but said it must have been a snipe. From then on it didn't matter if I approached the lake from upwind or downwind, stealthily or by surprise, the latte-coloured cannonbirds bolted over the water to the opposite shore, already safe before I could remember what to call them.

⌒

It's about how the lark in the bog is the one hand clapping. My feet are embedded and sodden. The squelching effort of advance is the lark's cue – while I'm shoegazing it erupts, a switch flicked upwards to on, an accent written perpendicular to the vowel of the world, a needle mending a rent in the air. I am an Icarus of mud, my sun having ascended, finding there is further yet to fall than ground.

⌒

Anna Karenina has something to say to you about swans. There's a pair that comes back every year to the Géaradh floodlands and settle onto the saucer-smooth water like two dollops of Chantilly cream, and I have no doubt they would have themselves for dessert if they could. It has never happened, but I

30

have a memory of them grooming each other some evening and forming a perfect heart with their necks while behind them a peach-coloured sky lets fall its drapery. The truth of the scene though is more sober. The closer you are, the slicker they glide; the slicker they glide, the further they get from you. And we all of us know how frantically things are working beneath the surface.

⁐

How does a swallow go? By coming, in the first place.

⁐

Leo Nikoláievich Tolstoy, born when the calendar was still in flux and no two regions could yet agree on what to call their units of time, could of course not have foreseen the kind of things we'd do – what would he make of me, for example, motionless before this picture-lamp of a laptop, this window with no world behind it, staring into it or out of it at a video of an owl that now gawks back, now slips behind the frame completely, whose little night music has been muted, whose image a modern man like me can only really hope to witness in this manner, second hand, before it disappears completely?

⁐

Things have got to the point with pigeons where their presence in the city is popularly resented but privately ignored, like daylight savings or another country's war. The reason for this is ubiquity. Pigeons in your day are punctuations in a block of text – apart from a very few exceptions you can expect them to populate it widely and at random; and of course it's the words of the day that call your attention, not the commas that fuss between them.

But then there was that drunken blur of a January in Venice, mist like anaesthetic. Against the stone of a piazza all the pigeons in unison, atoms of H_2 and O_2 in flow, and there am I in amongst it like a single drop of oil. I defy you not to notice a pigeon when it's in its hundreds and molten, pleating off from you like impact shockwaves in the ocean, where the comet has struck at the end of days.

Did all families have their own Rosie Robin? You know the one – she knew everything about you and betrayed your every experience to your mother, incredibly. Somewhere between dependence and independence, around the last time someone put you down having had you in their arms, Rosie simply lost interest – never spoke another word about you, found younger heroes, sweeter headlines. So now you're forced to make your own announcements.

And how does a cuckoo go? It goes like this: by going extinct.

I am telling you that all birds stay the same, go different. The tern for example is a bird like any other, but by flying pole to pole over the Earth in a fingernail curve, and never seeing the curl of its own breath against the cold, it doesn't winter. It sees more sun than any other thing, gets me half the year in light, cannot bear me at my worst.

And it's not just about the natives either. Smog over Santiago is like when in movies the cops drape a corpse in a white sheet: from where we stand, above and outside the crime scene, it seems redundant to obscure what we all know is there beneath, but we are grateful nonetheless for the gesture, the ritual. Someone points out a condor behind us, a 180 degree spin away from the city, and for the half-minute or so that we track it, this open parenthesis, across the sky, we recognise our own luck in life. Then the condor slides behind a mountain, like a card into an envelope, and mails itself into memory. We were so lucky, we tell ourselves, and continue our descent back out of nature.

(My father has found out what I am writing and asked me to include his two beloved chickens, Maura (the dowdier of the two) and Celeste (whose black, shellac-effect feathers make her look as if she has constantly just stepped out of the shower). They are horrid. Their feet are human feet defleshed; their wattles and combs are eczematic; they unbed flowers and scratch and screech for bread. That thing people say – about creatures being more scared of you than you of them – is wrong for Maura and Celeste, whose scuttling away has me in reeling in relief.)

And in what way does a pheasant go? Let me tell you: in a furore, with ado, rustling like one of those origami fortune-telling finger games, but on whose every wing is written *run for it,* and to which the only sensible response is laughter.

～

The hummingbird, so desperate for a quick exit, has learned, uniquely, to reverse.

～

Back to that Tolstoy quote, which I've translated after a few consultations with speakers of Slavic languages into what I think sounds best in English. There's no right answer, and I'm not the first to deliberate. Is it that all happy families are alike, or that they resemble each other? Is it each unhappy family, or all, or every? Are unhappy families unhappy in their own way, or do they just differ? Are birds? Do birds?

The goldfinch leaves Irish as *lasair choille,* as economic in its poetry as Bashō or Ungaretti. How do we go about dragging that (down?) into English? There's grammar to contend with, circling squares: English has no genitive case, so the neat *choille* will either fold down into a compound noun or stretch into a posessive noun phrase. This will give us the choice between forest-flame, or flame of the forest. Why forest and not woods? And anyway *lasair* is more blaze than flame. Are we talking the blaze of colour, or the blaze of transience?

This has all got away from me. Look, the bird is bright. We call it as we see it.

～

The seagull leaves with a chip in its mouth, and my Dub with a chip on his shoulder.

⁂

Pelagic outside the breeding season. So birds ghost too, then. The shearwater has its fun, lives up to its name until the time comes to land again.

⁂

For some project or other you would later abandon, you wanted to study a peacock up close. The plan of that Sunday was to go to the Japanese gardens, smoke a joint under the witch-fingered maple, you sketching the peacocks, me not writing cause I can't do it if you're looking at me. So I sank into overthought there on the perfect moss, felt ugly and guileless and gauche, couldn't seem to land a joke. It suddenly became vital to me to steal a peacock feather for you, on first thought because I figured it would make me seem more butch, and on second because if the first thought failed, then at least the feather would be a memento of the day, of me inside the day, its gas-flame eye unblinking and and absolutely disallowing oblivion.

I couldn't get close enough to the peacock. Between my advance and his retreat, I believe the distance between us never grew nor diminished, just kept to that of the proverbial ten-foot pole, with which neither of us could touch the other. Though one of us, desperately, was trying.

⁂

How does a starling go? I'll tell you now: in plural, and over again.

⁂

And how does a corncrake go? You'll only know this once it's gone, but soundlessly. You can't miss it.

⌒

There's a very smart poem called '13 Ways of Looking at a Blackbird' by Wallace Stevens which gets taught quite widely, and rightly so. But he misses a trick, I think, in not clarifying whether the bird he means is really a blackbird, or a type of blackbird, since blackbird as a word is quite schematic and could just as well mean raven or jackdaw or rook or chough or crow or carrion crow or hooded crow or what have you. A better poem would be 13 Ways of Looking at 13 Types of Blackbird, but that's 169 total viewpoints of departure and I understand if he couldn't bear to write it. You have to draw the line somewhere.

⌒

Wrens go from me in this way: abdication.

Erratics

They told me this might happen.
It's textbook – a belly of ice
impresses its weight on rock, contracts,
expands, wrests chinks in armour open,
grunts its U's and V's and passes
on, slick from the act.

Around are drumlins, the littlest aftermath,
glad of the scrub. Eskers, languid, spent,
cirques that yawn in high morale.
For the sore-thumb boulder, though, the ugly truth
is just that here a glacier made its dark descent,
opened its cold hand, and let fall.

Two Silverbirches

for Mom and Dad

Text, in this part of the world,
linguistically, this is thus
so this tree undoes winter first,
difference. You could set
full green pashmina here,
though we don't need science
communicate underground
— essentially linking
The paper-tear of
long before it presents; wind
is printed on the other.
will scroll in three-week time
and the second letting fall
last soil-song in the round, one last.
Seen from the other side, of course,
that writes the root, and the full stop
It doesn't matter.
nonsense.

is read from left to right. Psycho-
how we visualise time,
then this one. Three weeks'
your watch to it:
this one still knitting. Science,
to tell us, tells us that they
through filaments called hyphae
pinkies under our driveway.
a distant car is stealthily imparted
barely scans one, but its gaze
Last rights, I'd bet this house,
too, the first already deafening
all its ears to the ground. One
kick-back to Ireland.
this is all reversed, and it's the bud
casts the sentence.
One read without the other:

Fás Aon Oíche

I am monster-green by psychology
so I can't help it if I didn't take it well
when it dawned on me where you'd been
and whom, more to the point, you'd been in.

One-night stand was the excuse, and
that's not a red line, but my mind
went straight to the ink-cap in Irish, swelling
like a nocturne into a warm, new world.

Slievemore / An Sliabh Mór / The Big Mountain

SLIEVEMORE

Not just any mountain
(in metres, all told, not even that),
Slievemore is cetacean in memory.
It never soared; it surfaced.

Every summer, some mainlander
would mistake weather for climate
and scale it in a dry spell,
unready for the heavy hand of mist
that inevitably fell and swept
them off it like whatever was left
of the bread from the breakfast table.

AN SLIABH MÓR

I've ridden others.
I'm not talking mountain-
range numbers of mountains,
but mountains enough
for comparison.
Mountains with main character strut,
background mountains,
greener mountains, browner.
I've broken some mountains in,
been broken back in by some mountains.
I have palmed escarpments
to tameness,
I've drawn ridges
up into themselves,

given form sometimes
to arêtes
with just one look.
I've clung to mountains
that gave no purchase
to the spur, dumb mountains,
mountains covered in dust,
mountains that buck on fault lines and
mountains, in the end,
that were not worth mustering.
The worst thing to find is
that the first one, all this time,
was enough.

THE BIG MOUNTAIN

A field of bog cotton
at the big mountain's foot
nods in deference,
in surrender and
in unison,
a scattering of Catholics at sea.
Not just any mountain. The.

Changeling

Easier than getting into
what sex was, I guess,
was to tell the cagier
children that the new baby
had washed up on the beach
with the seaweed.

Easier, and no less true:
even now, I don't sleep well at all
and my go-to is to play dead
on a bed of egg-wrack
and wait for that night's sea
to drag me back where I belong.

Synecdoche

The man from O'Mahoney's
Tree Services Ltd. says that the only
difference between himself and an arborist
is softer hands and clout.
He recommends felling, to no one's surprise.

For all we know he's right, filling
his boots with Mom's brown bread, though
I find his further grounds
overkill: *comes a storm*, says he,
this Cúil Aodha Cassandra,

comes a storm and it's through
your windshield you'll find it.
Or through your eye, God forbid.
And the masterstroke: *Or through some young thing.*
That settles it for Mom.

June that same year and the grasshoppers
are all saying *heat*. I emerge
from the dead-still lake in a film
of scum and water striders to the far-off wasping
of a chainsaw, and march home towards it.

I am in time for the fall,
the tree genuflecting to its own expiry
and the leading-lady swoon of the leaves on the ground
like all its life's breath had arrived at once.
We stand over what's left, a halo

of sawdust around what looks, from above,
like a map of a city – old town
in the centre; high-rise splinters
to the side where it was tipped; monochrome,
but only if you squint and from this far up.

Zoom out further, and in a time
before cities there was real fatalism
and risk was an afterthought, quotidian.
If something killed you, it killed you –
there would be other lives.

A Butterfly Struggles Against Coastal Winds, 5 Metres Offshore

Whatever the before
    (how had it flown out so far?
    what for?)
and whatever the after
    (Did one of those circling seagulls
    pluck it out of clean air
    when we weren't looking?
    Did it stop beating its wings
    briefly enough to thud like
    a closed book on the ceiling of the sea?),
I think that for however short a moment
    (on a Wednesday, 4ish,
    in spite of all that fucking wind,
    and in spite of an ocean
    the sound of shredding pages)
we made it hold its place in the sky
just by wanting it to.
Something one of us, I know,
    could not have done alone.

Pornography for Trees

search for: XYLEM
    TROPISM
    ABSCISSION
    CORK
    POLLARDING
    FRUIT DROP
    OSMOSIS
    VENATION

BROADLEAF LIKE PIANO
PLAYER'S HAND

RADICAL ARAUCARIA
TAKES NO PRISONERS,
EARNS ITS NAME

NO PROTECTION! YOU
GET WHAT PLAGUES YOU
GET

BRUTAL HEAT –
DROUGHT HAS WHOLE
FOREST IN CHOKEHOLD

THIS ANIMAL IS AT YOUR
BECK AND CALL FOR
SEED DISPERSAL

FREELOADER LICHEN
TAKING ADVANTAGE

MASTIC OOZES
WITHOUT SHAME AS
OTHERS WATCH ON
WITHOUT SHAME

NEEDLES ON CONIFER
LIKE PIANO PLAYER'S
FINGERS

TALLEST / OLDEST /
THICKEST / MOST
VIOLENT / CUTEST /
CREEPIEST / MOST
PROLIFIC... RECORDS
COMPILATION 2

COQUETTE COROLLA
SAVES ITSELF FOR RIGHT
TIME, UNFOLDS

WIND LICKS BIRCH
COPPICE
(SMR)

SPECIES CAN AUTO-
POLLINATE, WATCH IF
YOU DON'T BELIEVE

YOU WON'T BELIEVE THE
TRICK THESE
MANGROVES HAVE FOR
SIFTING OUT
SALTWATER...

ETHICLESS SEX!
MILLIONS OF TREES ARE
IN YOUR AREA, WAITING.

On Falling

Falling, first of all, is the natural state of things, not sideways
progress, or advance or rise. Powerpoints on grammar and marketing
use horizontal arrows to show the way things go, erroneously,
and that image of life as a long-slog trudge across to some eventual
Stage Right is also wrong – the arrow should point down,
and life is not theatre; it's sport, if falling were a sport. Steer your axis
clockwise and you have it. Falling is how the bullet moves
from chamber to barrel; it's the express fall of the bullet
that tears man down into meat, and the tin can into a colander.
Rugby referees yell: *Touch Crouch Pause Engage*, and set the players
to falling, and shoulders of ice in Arctic ice-floes fall
in the same way, contesting every inch on the face (not the surface)
of what is there. The dog that drags you after scent is falling.
To the wheely suitcase you are anchor, not chauffeur.
St. Patrick's Day floats fall. So do earthworms after rain,
which falls the truest. So do bowling balls. So did every road
that ever led to Rome. Falling is the lot of rivers.

This is not even to talk of gravity, although we must. Gravity is brought
home to me on Inis Mór today – the cliffs are all right angles,
which somehow heightens everything. A high, indifferent sun.
The Atlantic, indifferent. Clints of limestone laid out neat as Tetris,
and hot as a griddle under my thighs. My feet over the edge.
I can't stop thinking about what it means to lose someone,
mothers on hearing tough news that slump to the old, loose lino,
the most ordinary of movements. Only a foot or so from the sofa
to the floor, the easiest foot ever fallen. I have fallen,
and the sea is in on it, sawing at the cliff-base to quicken the last drop.
And it would be easy: the pixels of light below me on the water
are the smallest measurements of time and the largest
measurements of number; they come and go. They don't

agonise over it. A shower of gannets is knifing the sea.
They'll go blind from this, and don't mind. Ahead of me,
a fishing boat is slipping into the fine slit of the horizon.

Irish Elk *(Megaloceros giganteus)*

It's not enough to stand
an adult man beside it
for comparison:

that's fair neither to the elk
nor the man. You have to put
yourself in its hooves,

set its factory of blood
back into business.
Do the rutting that has to be

done; there's more where that
came from. You have to imagine
the elk extant,

a tree of an animal:
not dead. Just wintering.

Professional Earth

I am professional earth:
earth that works
for a living.

⁓

Professional earth, by which I mean
I don't do this for fun. I don't provide
the mise-en-scène for the
stupid operas of cattle
because they chew the scenery so well.
I am not stage, fourth wall
and audience in one just for my health.
What good is a bouquet thrown
if then it's eaten?
I do this
because this is what is done.

⁓

Since it's all the same to the clouds what they grunt above,
I'm professional earth.

⁓

Strictly professional, in that
earth doesn't talk and therefore doesn't talk
back. It isn't called anything,
doesn't call anything. It doesn't lie;
it lies there. It puts nothing into words.
Repeating is not peat that says again.
If it can't tell, then it can't tell
on you. I will take you to your grave.

Professional earth is nothing
for something.

⌒

The weight of a calf carried and a calf given birth to is knowable. The weight of grass in winter versus grass in spring must be knowable. Like the weight of yesterday's rain and the rain of the day before that and the weight of the two combined and on top of each other. Knowable must be the weight of a bull in heat, the bull relieved. The weight of forty seeds, and then the weight of the forty cabbages reaped. The weight of the space where forty cabbages have been. The weight of machinery. Someone must know the weight of dew minus the weight of dew when someone has dragged their feet through it. The weight of prey inside the weight of predator. It is objective. The weight of the arrived-at morning, and then in an hour or so, the weight of the burnt-off morning. The weight of the hungry man, the weight of the fed man, his weight when he's half-cut and bursting, his weight when he's passed water, the weight of water in a man, the weight of his fist inside a cow, the weight of that same fist, pulled out. Even before it was weighed, known was the weight of a torc, a thousand harvests down, and the weight of its wearer, passed through a worm and better for it. The weight of the worm, the constellation of worms, the worm hoard, the parliaments of worms, the great unwashed, the unheard of and unherdable droves of worms, the floating voter worms, the schools of worms, the schools of thoughts of worms, the thoughts of worms, the weight of these: knowable. All knowable.
There's a god. There's got to be.

⌒

I am. All the snow in the world might obscure it, but I do exist.

It is what it is and we are what we are and there is very little hope
of this ever changing.

⤳

I am professional earth.
There are cathedrals of fern
at my edges. There are hedge-row
chorus-lines. Buds ejaculate
out of reach, incessantly.
(Treemen, the locals call it
jokingly, proudly.)
Pride parades of growth,
messy and profligate.
There are Carmen Mirandas
all the way along,
everything's rococo.
There is uncontrollable laughter.
I keep schtum:
I'm professional.

⤳

Advice for earth in apprenticeship: keep your head down;
sleep only in the abstract, not in winter; don't light up
and don't extinguish; practice all your vices: smoke,
drink, use, gorge, hoard, covet, fuck, get fucked;
don't you breathe a single word of this to anyone;
shoulder your lot like a Catholic; alter your makeup
to incorporate, also, the man-made; bear muck;
bear weight; leave their claims of greenery in tact;
forget you're nature.

Caol le Caol agus Leathan le Leathan

That language submits to the will of its speakers
is perfect in that it is flawed –
it's a hard thing to learn that the sounds that are slender
must distance themselves from the broad.

The Salmon of Knowledge

The poet Finegas said
    that he had waited 7 years to capture
    this one fish: whose finest bone
    if plucked would sing the known
    world's musics; the sweeping gesture
    of whose dorsal fin could articulate
    the night's stars; whose nut-round mouth
    had all language in it; about
    whose tongue hung words that made the dumb articulate;
    whose little eye had spied
    everything, everything; whose little heart
    had burst and shrunk, had had the arts
    of love done unto it, so knew them from the out, from inside;
    whose skin both shone
    and bore reflection.

We, though. We know it was Cú Chulainn who ended up
eating the fish in question. So Finegas continued:
    that it was beyond the edge of measure
    in what way rain would fall were it not water,
    what clouds would then do with themselves;
    that, like so, what's lost is knowable, but what's never had is not;
    that the weight of him-plus-fish was more than just himself,
    so he would now press less heavily into the earth: another upshot;
    that eating was a two-way thing, and only the hunger
    was his and his alone; that he had after all some small science,
    the more of which learned, the older the learner,
    the more asked of him, the less free; and that since
    he had known all along this knowledge would not be his,
    he could afford once again to covet it, this time even harder;
    and that 7 years is nothing; that a poet's patience is
    not for knowledge, but for good words, in good order.

The Geata Dearg

A hundred yards would be about from here to the Geata Dearg, or
She said she was at the Geata Dearg before it dawned on her

are shibboleths, but not ones so grand as 'shibboleth' intimates:
it's just shorthand, a little shop-talk that shopping here permits,

that for Dad is a means of exaggerating the nearness or farness
of a thing, for Pat Browne his field's entrance, for us a tennis

net during Wimbledon. We don't even know if the red in its name
is for its one-time paint or present rust, if it lacks colour or needs some,

but I've said it more often than most of my English.
I came out of this world, not into it.

Magpie

Some creatures value the human, take
a shine to the colour blue, for example, even though blue
things neither nourish or preserve them; even so, make

blue their life's work, seek it out, build keepsake
shrines from scraps of denim, spearmint wrappers, For You From Corfu
tat, the marzipan balloons on a gender reveal cake;

some creatures mean *boy*, some more mean *girl;* some mean *earthquake*
when seen on higher ground, which means they have abandoned you;
some hold funerals for their dead, some undertake

to divvy up the dead one's blue things; some would call you snowflake
if you flinched at this, since some are so inured to death that death
    is déjà vu;
some know ritual for bullshit, but perform it anyway, for
    performance sake;

some consume as performance: whatever bread there is to break,
    they break,
no matter if it's steak or carrion, songless bug or songbird –
    nothing's off the menu
for some creatures; some creatures would sooner bite the hand
    than bear the handshake;

some themselves are blue; they might not break
this news until they're seen in flight, a sky-tattoo;
some creatures, like tattoos, are a mistake.
Take the magpie for example. Take it.

Warry Loomph

i.m. Mary Riordan

The next to last
speaker dies, and the language dies

and it is down to
the one man left behind
so
to boil it in with his oats,
wash his hands with
it. It,

the folderol of
talk, will not long
outlast the tongue talking it,
once let go. Even
so,
he vacuums the floors to
himself, shovels snow
untranslatably, tries
nightly to have enough

slept for the next
day's object-
less keening, mountain-
less echo.

For the birds, might as well be.
They too
will die from something.

Blueballs

I have to bite my lip when he asks me
– 5 hours, an ocean, a split-second
delay, and half a language behind –
what this idiom means, but I think I get it across by
using the politest terms I have to hand:
the words *relieve* and *appetite*,
the merest hint of a fist gesture.

Turns out he meant the flowers,
but the basic principle still stands –
imagine, Jorge, that you're dead.
The earth has eaten you, your beautiful eyes.
You're in blackness, not just darkness,
clenched tight as a blood-clot,
when, I don't know, through photosynthesis
or pheromones I guess, a message gets down to you:
Up here is a warm place. Something in you says
yes, and you stalk upwards, easing into
open-air display. The warm hand of light
draws out a pale bud, then a caravan, more brightly.

It's downhill from there
and you slip like the flag of an old country
back into pastel, flecked with dirt,
quite a bit more than just a penny spent.

Elegy for an Eel, in Advance

Elegy – because in this moment you have no inkling that you'll die, but you will die.
Advance – since forward and foreword are homophones in some dialects.
Eel – according to the *Oxford Dictionary of Etymology,* comes: *from Proto-Germanic *ælaz, which is of unknown origin.*
For, an, in, and a comma – because these, like some other squiggles I know, might seem immaterial in the grand scheme of things, but aren't.

⌒

All coincidence begins and ends
in the Lee being my nearest river,

your mirror. But language isn't astrology,
nor neatness kismet:

you aren't bound for me.
You're somewhere off Bermuda

you're an eyelash in the Gulf Stream,
too far down even for torchlight.

And what? Are you really so slick
as to thread every eye and sneak past every trawler

in the Atlantic?
To get to where I am,

behind a dam, which is itself
behind another dam,

in circumferences of chance,
I give you a snowball's.

Plus you'd have to really want to.
I doubt you do. I understand that

there is no such thing as a river
too good to pass up.

Rusalka, Selkie, Sedna, Varun, Clann Lir,
Bäckahästen, Mul Gwishin, Bunyip, Leviathan,
Siren, Pincoya, Poseidon, Noah, Styx …
Whoever's mythology got water right,
I wish you theirs.

Skellig List

Look at him there in his canities,
his nape like Skellig Michael's ombré
cliff-face, greying with the faeces
of half the north Atlantic's puffins. Sombre-

coloured elsewhere too, so any
beauty there might be has few beholders.
That he can be fat is uncanny,
given he is thin, and he looks older

than you might remember him:
to whom it may concern, David Nash
is unattached and treading water. Hymns
are sung to greater catches

so simpler rhymes are sufficient here,
since he's also overshot the sonnet.
That's false modesty: he thinks the sea heavier
for having him on it.

The Opposite of a Cow

Io – as far as I have gathered from the myth –
was turned into a cow for being too beautiful.
Avarice like this I shouldn't understand, but do:
the grasses in the high field this evening are
graceful, stentorian, fine, and unified in movement,
a school of air-mackerel. Cultures love gold because
it's pliant and brilliant; my grasses here comply with gold.
Whatever's green comes only to foot-height; hand-height
I am palming the beards of grass-heads, sleepy and seed-heavy.
They are, as a whole, untouchable: as one too much,
as many too many, the peacock's hundred eyes
and my human two are unworthy of witness. Better
that the grass of this dusk be made cud of; better
it pass through, better it turn into, the cow which is its opposite.

Ill Wind

after the Mapuzungun of Lionel Lienlaf

Across the stump fields,
desperate, panting,
the wind turns back on itself,

a labrador duped
by the dummy throw.
It unhinges then,

can't fathom there's a world
unholdable in its teeth,
a bird's nest it can't bracket.

Turlough

Water with its moon in Libra:
now you see it,

sudden water, where yesterday
you'd happened

on a desire path
home, which would have halved

the time it takes. Now with water,
doubled. Doubled water –

the lake you see before you now is
the lake you don't

inverted, the water table
with its legs in the air,

an underground overed,
a frown upside-downed.

You roll up your jeans
to ford or afford it, and exactly at waist

height you are one of two things:
an anchor tethering sky

or the lake's space programme.
This water one day

will leave land in its wake.
You will stand in

a grass meniscus
while the water, untroubled,

summers in closure.
Now you don't.

All Square at Half-Time in the Mid-Cork Junior A Football Quarter Final between Canovee and Grenagh, Inniscarra GAA Grounds, 21st of August 2022

Something like the title of a poem
that rivals in itself the poem's length, I want them
to keep going, take heart in their parity,
and draw forever. It's unbearable, all this hope,
yet 30-something men must bear it
and play more. Sport makes extra time
in that event, in a crack at infinity.
There are Hail Marys, yes. And there are matrices
with fewer permutations, although it's also simple:
at each whistle, start again, make more decisions.
It means you're strong if you hold out
and hold your ground, but we don't go
for hero-worship – a muttered *Dhera, milk
would turn faster than Eoin O'Driscoll* gets a laugh, since
at this stage of the game, that's all you can do.

To Divine Water

O first god or greatest, man
has made carbon
copies, has dreamt up Poseidon
and Mohammad, but has not
outdone you.
It's in the absentee's
armoury to haunt, and so here
you aren't. Your mass is
constant; there is as much
of you as always,
but you are now spread
thicker on another land's
bread, while
all is only flour here.
This is hard to stomach.

There is rain. Not long-winded
as before, more post-it note
than post,
but you write that you are, still,
and the aftermath is
bank-holiday-sweet –
the rivers, hungover, in sprawl and
capped with surf.
Man is persuaded this will tide
him over. Man is not calling
that bluff. But then: dust.
Then, again, the empty bed.
It starts to sink in with the forest,
which mints its coppers
for circulation, and concedes.
Man dances.

Man haggles with the ghost,
spells WATER with the ouija lens,
consults with Pisces ascending,
says *water*, finally,
really means it.

I hold the Y of the hazel in
my hands, and partake in sham.
The up-down jerk
of the wood, like
the kneel-stand-kneel
of what's left of the congregation,
is a kind of amen.

Bog Butter

Uncle John in his bachelor's plot, some time in the 70s,
slicing out turf enough to do him for the winter, a little
extra maybe that he'd sell down in Purteen harbour.
His peat-spade hits on a softness different
from the normal softness: bog butter
in a slab, the imprint of muslin still on the tell-tale pale
like sock elastic, had been lurking mute as a planet
since the Bronze Age. Hauls his butter-baby home,
catches whiting to fry in a slick of it (*Mighty!* apparently),
then donates what's left to the National Museum.
The island, they tell him, is likely studded
with hundreds of these, but actually to find one
is like catching a balloon launched upwards from history.
They put it in a glass box, museum lamplight,
little placard explaining the discovery, though not
the discoverer. At his shoulders tourists and schoolgroups,
John anonymous among them, and the great albino tuna
that had swum into his life suspended forever, mighty,
so very briefly his, but once his.

The Freshwater Pearl Mussel Project ©

We here at the Project
get it. The mussel is hard sell.
We tried first with the science –

margaritifera margaritifera
is a long-living invertebrate bivalve mollusc
capable of fostering pearls –

but really who has the patience?
We can't sex them up much either,
save maybe to note how its one aperture

is decidedly vaginal,
or that they detonate sperm like champagne
in the cup-winners' dressing room.

Have we got your attention?
Allow us then to lose it: the pearl
mussel needs a favour

and does itself none. It is
as fussy as a princeling – the river has to be
the kind of water

rivers aren't anymore – see-through,
sterling. The sperm must carry,
convene with the egg mid-stream like two sub-

plots resolving, then suspend.
From here god-willing to the gills of
this one particular trout, where they encyst

and then drop off, splat as figs,
9 months later into the silt.
5 more years like so in further

wait, honing the pearl
and quickening once more the pearl
necklace. Sperm in the water.

We will not keep you much longer.
We know that you have other
irons in the fire and this

might all be hard for you to hear.
We're not asking for a pearl
mussel-shaped tear, just a full

reversal of the way that all things are.
In the spirit of full disclosure:
it's been the royal *we* all this time.

Observations in the Field of Elders

(i)
The crown formation
of a raindrop on impact: the fruit of the cloud.
The stop-motion fireworks
of elderflowers in July: the cloud of the fruit.

(ii)
A nugget from the lottery of naming:
the Irish *trom* is both
elder and burden, and this
is pronounced like a learner of German
(though not an actual German)
would say *dream.*

(iii)
I'm getting drunk
because six months ago I packed a bottle of gin
with elderfowers and sugar
and stored it in a cool dark place
as a small taste of summer for my future self,
and also because
I have the time it takes to drink it
before this jumper, returned,
smells only of me once more.

Amhrán na mBréag, or The Grass is Blue

after Dolly Parton

Black is not the absence of colour; it is all colour in convergence.
Before enlightenment, black people in Irish were *an cine gorm,*
the blue folk.
History is not the only thing written by victors.
In Norway in winter, the navy given off by banks of snow often
outdoes the lightboxes prescribed by doctors.
Physics is poetry dragged down to fact.
Saudade, the Atlantic-coloured knot of longing, is untranslatable.
Mussolini was the better artist of the two.
Pink was for boys, first.
Religion is belief; atheism still belief.
The hottest flame is azure, no matter how you pronounce it.
Ignorance is wasted on the dumb.
It is fair that the price of one eye should be another eye.
If a thing is naturally red, it is because it wants to kill you, or
feed you, or be fed.
The blood inside you is not red.
Brecht said: 'Eating comes first; then morals.'
There is nothing new under the sun.
'They fuck you up, your Mum and Dad.'
The cooler reaches of the colour wheel in Irish are chaos, are
Irish in chaos: anything can be anything – the grass blue, the
clouds green. Nothing is grey.
Querer es poder.
The only way you'll learn is by heart.
The number of stripes (cerulean and whitewash white) in the
flag of Greece represents the number of syllables in that
country's motto - Ελευθερία ή θάνατος – liberty or death.
Since you left me, you have often doubted yourself in the night.

You can tell teal apart from turquoise more easily if you speak Russian.

The more you know …

Character is fate. Grammar is hindsight.

Some of the above is untrue.

In my experience the world, indeed, is sometimes flat.

Potato (a biography)

DISCOVERY
Chiloe, Chile, 1566

The fathomless sea. I wanted to say to someone
my God the sea. I came to the other side of it for under-
standing, for something to rhyme with my awe.
There is, after all, both a me and an I in America. Here,
trees called *pewen* hang over the world like
quotation marks. Its nut is good and nutritious.
Today the locals gave me a potato, and my hand
was surely designed to hold it. It has the curve
of a beach in miniature, it is brown as a farmer's nape.
The native gods are brutal, but their world is new.

DEPENDENCE
Skibbereen, County Cork, 1815

God's gift. You can't blame us for loving a sun
that pounds inside the earth. It is everything rye and butter
aren't. The fish-clotted sea is impassive and we draw
from it, but the saltwater curls to a smirk; every year
it draws dozens of us down as collateral. The cows we milk
are not worth independence either. So out of nowhere, this
new protuberance, this hunk of luck, fattened
to our particular moisture. The foodstuff we deserve.
How could we not love it? It could usurp the grain, rape
this land of all variety, and we would say thank you.

DISEASE
Skibbereen, County Cork, 1847

Full moon above the ground, new moon below it, new moon
in the stomach. A debt to light is the remainder.
How snatchable defeat is from the jaw,
how conspicuous are objects when they move to souvenir.
The white flower soils. The stubborn sea recoils unsportsmanlike
and here is death. And here. The eyewitness
accounts are all the same: the story of the unmanned
man, the body that's been minused of a body; nerves
that bear no message to the brain and drape
like wool over the ribs and heart. So here is death. Here, too.

DEPARTURE
New York, 1870

Back in America, and everyone who eats is Anglophone.
I change. I wretch and throw my tongue into the water,
if that is what you want. Such is hunger. Raw
meat in the new world can't be chooser, travels in steer-
age. *Amhdhorchacht*, raw darkness, means nothing here. I lick
it from memory until it blandens into uselessness.
New language gives me a blight-black sea, a secondhand
sea, a sea that won't lenite, a gruel-grey sea, a sea that serves
me right for all that hubris. My mouth makes the shape
of the sea. My tongue and teeth make do.

DEPENDENCE
Canovee, County Cork, 2020

Dad out the back in the potato drills. Grandson
in tow, affecting his stoop. For both this is a matter
of establishment: what it means to have a *grá*
for a thing or a person. The pike turns and potatoes appear
like foetuses, like fists in victory, the stuff of life in cyclic
miniature. For culture, somehow, this matters to us.
Say its name three times into a mirror, and
there I'll be, in duty to the rights that it reserves.
Incessant sea, you are planted in my landscape;
I wash my heart in the wake of you.

Caoineadh

I'll whisht soon I promise,
but first: a little grief.
Different, though, from the species
of keening we know, for if
I were to keen in print,
I would rightly be cancelled
a posteriori. By dint
of being dead, or at least old,
its will takes precedence
over mine to resurrect it.
So how do you lament
lament, then? To whom? For whose benefit?

Soon I'll whisht I promise, soon.

Why You Should Really Think About Rewilding

We are standing
in what used to be
our forest.
Some *spailpín* rot or
spore of fungus
had ridden here on
a swallow's wing, or stowed
itself in the fine suede deckshoes of
exotic seamen,
had somehow anyway
come upon a needle, got
sucked up and drawn
into the heartwood, and the heartwood
had played vector to the rot,
which spurted out in turn
hemophilically along
the tree internet like
fast-forward sap, and we know
from there how things
go south:
our wide-eyed jungle
died.
I understand all that.
What I don't accept is
why we couldn't
just have let it pass away
like everything else does:
slouching and faintly
and bewildered and
milky and drifting and slow-motion sap-slow,
not
bluntly, like this stump-scape
no man's land.

If we'd left the place
as was,
it might even have outlived us.
Anyhow the land
isn't good for anything else, so
look at us standing here now,
already ankle-deep in thickets
keen as kitten claws
and shrub reclaiming, dogged
as truth.
This is an overture, it
establishes the main
themes that get recalled
later on
in the thick of
the story.
Groundwork is a memory
posting itself forward in time,
so you needn't lift a finger –
it is its own device.
What I'm saying is
take a chance on it.
The seed is reckless.

NOTES

p.13   'Lámh' is the Irish word for hand, and also the name of a type of Irish Sign Language

p. 22   Hy Brasil is an apocryphal island that appears on some medieval maps off the west coast of Ireland.

p. 40   'Fás Aon Oíche' (lit. one night's growth) is one of the names in Irish for ink-cap mushrooms.

p. 54   'Caol le Caol agus Leathan le Leathan'. Literally 'slender with slender and broad with broad', a maxim to help schoolchildren to remember the rules of vowel harmony in Irish.

p. 55   The Salmon of Knowledge is a myth about an elusive salmon which bestowed infinite knowledge and wisdom on whomsoever managed to catch and eat it.

p. 56   Geata Dearg simply means 'red gate'.

p. 58   Warry Loomph is the Yabi word for lonesome. Yabi is a language my father and aunt made up.

p. 62   A Skellig List was/is a poetic form (often purely oral) from Cork and Kerry, composed to shame or make fun of single people, or for the purposes of matchmaking. This would be composed and recited on Ash Wednesday before the sun set over the Skelligs (the westernmost point), as marriages could not be performed again before Easter Sunday.

p. 74   'Amhrán na mBréag, or The Grass is Blue'. An Amhrán na mBréag ('song of lies') was a poetic form in which the author simply listed untruths.

p. 79   'Canoineadh'. A lament or dirge (keen/keening) in Irish tradition. A complex set of protocols, such as the structure of the caoineadh, or the taboo of repeating its content, meant most communities had a designated, experienced woman or group of women to perform them at funerals.

www.ingramcontent.com/pod-product-compliance
Lightning Source LLC
Chambersburg PA
CBHW030500100426
42813CB00002B/293